Budget Hacks: Practical Savings Strategies for Real People

Guide to Getting Ahead From a Frugal Mother of 8 That Did It on One Income

Publisher BeeLovedHolm
ISBN 978-1-963278-03-3
February 2024

BeeLovedHolm

Table of Contents: Navigation Station: Plotting Your Journey Through the Pages

Introduction: Frugal Wisdom from a Seasoned Family Navigator

Growing up as the oldest of seven children and later raising eight of my own, I understand the intricate dance of budgeting and stretching funds. With both my father and husband serving as the sole providers for our families, frugality became a way of life. Here, I share insights and lessons learned from a life shaped by making every dollar count:

- Growing up in a large family taught me the importance of resourcefulness and creativity to meet the needs of many without overspending.
- In both my childhood home and my own family, having only one breadwinner required strategic financial planning and wise budgeting.
- Embracing a frugal lifestyle doesn't mean sacrificing quality. It's about making intentional choices that prioritize value and longevity.
- Passed down from my parents and refined through the years, the art of being frugal became a family tradition and a valuable skill.
- The journey of navigating financial challenges has honed my ability to find creative solutions, from

crafting homemade items to discovering budget-friendly alternatives.

- As a mother and grandmother, I've passed on the legacy of thriftiness to the next generation, instilling the importance of financial thoughtfulness.
- Balancing the budget requires a delicate dance between needs and wants, finding harmony in providing for the family's essentials without compromising on quality of life.
- Living well doesn't have to be synonymous with extravagant spending. It's about finding joy in simple pleasures and maximizing the value of every dollar.
- I share these insights with the hope that they become guiding stars for others navigating the seas of family finance, offering practical wisdom for a more financially secure and fulfilling life.

My journey has been one of constant learning, adapting, and discovering new ways to make the most of limited resources. Each lesson has added a layer of resilience to the fabric of our frugal lifestyle.

May these lessons resonate with you, serving as beacons of frugality and wisdom on your financial journey. Remember, it's not just about the dollars saved; it's about the life lived with intention and purpose.

Chapter I: Thrifty Traditions: Navigating the Seas of Family Finance

A. Prices Going Up Faster Than Income

In a world where the cost of living seems to outpace income growth, families on a limited budget face an uphill battle. This book delves into the financial challenges encountered by these families and explores the importance of reevaluating spending habits for long-term financial well-being.

B. Purpose of the Book

1. **Empowering Families to Make Strategic Financial Decisions**

In the quest for financial freedom, strategic decision-making is key. This book aims to empower families by providing insights into how they can navigate the complex landscape of personal finance.

2. **Encouraging a Mindset Shift towards Thoughtful Spending**

Shifting from a consumer-driven mindset to one focused on thoughtful spending is crucial. The book offers practical advice on cultivating this shift, ensuring that every financial decision aligns with long-term goals.

3. **Providing Practical Tips for Maximizing Limited Resources**

With limited resources at their disposal, families need actionable strategies. This book equips readers with practical tips to make the most of what they have, promoting efficiency in financial management.

C. Scope of the Book

1. **Budgeting Fundamentals**

Budgeting is the foundation of financial success. We explore practical budgeting strategies tailored to limited incomes, emphasizing the importance of tracking expenses and setting realistic financial goals.

2. **Lifestyle Adjustments**

Embracing a frugal yet fulfilling lifestyle is a key component of financial freedom. This book guides readers through making intentional lifestyle adjustments without compromising on happiness and well-being.

3. **Building Financial Resilience**

Financial setbacks are inevitable. This section introduces the concept of financial resilience, teaching families how to weather unexpected storms by creating emergency funds and building a robust financial safety net.

4. **Practical Money-Saving Strategies**

The heart of thoughtful spending lies in adopting money-saving habits. This book offers a plethora of practical, easy-to-implement strategies sourced from financial experts and real-life success stories.

II. The Thoughtful Spending Mindset

Before delving into specific strategies, it's crucial to understand the philosophy behind thoughtful spending. This mindset is not about deprivation; rather, it's a conscious decision to allocate resources in a way that aligns with one's values and long-term goals.

A. **Understanding Thoughtful Spending**

1. Thoughtful spending is about making intentional choices with each purchase.
2. It involves evaluating the value a purchase brings to your life, beyond its immediate gratification.

B. **Breaking Free from Consumer Culture**

1. Consumer culture often drives impulse buying; thoughtful spending encourages breaking free from these habits.
2. By distinguishing between wants and needs, families can regain control over their financial destiny.

C. **Practicing Gratitude in Spending**

1. Cultivating gratitude for what you have helps in curbing the desire for unnecessary purchases.
2. Careful spending is a thoughtful gratitude practice, aligning purchases with a sense of appreciation.

III. Cultivating Thoughtful Spending Habits

Now equipped with a thoughtful spending mindset, let's delve into actionable strategies that will transform your financial landscape.

A. **Strategic Purchases**

1. **Delayed Gratification Technique**
    - Avoid impulsive purchases by employing a 24-hour rule: wait a day before making a non-essential purchase. During this time look at other options. I bought things and then found a better deal later that day.
2. **Value-Driven Purchases**
    - Assess the long-term value of a purchase rather than its immediate appeal.
    - Prioritize spending on experiences and items that contribute to your well-being. In five years from now, is this something that would have enhanced your life?

B. **Financial Accountability**

1. **Weekly Financial Check-Ins**
    - Set aside time each week to review your spending and adjust your budget accordingly.
2. **Accountability Partnerships**
    - Share financial goals with a trusted friend or family member for added support and motivation. Empowered with a thoughtful spending mindset and practical strategies, families on limited budgets can navigate the financial challenges of a world where prices rise faster than incomes. This book serves as a guide, encouraging readers to take control of their financial destiny through intentional, value-driven decisions. As we continue this journey towards financial freedom, remember: that every thoughtful choice brings you one step closer to a future of financial well-being.

Chapter 2: "The Millionaire Next Door Mindset: Unveiling the Secrets of True Wealth"

Before we dive into the heart of this book, I would like to share some profound wisdom shared by the authors of a groundbreaking work, "The Millionaire Next Door."[1] This masterpiece unravels the lifestyles of millionaires who, despite their immense wealth, didn't flaunt it. Let's peek into their mindset and uncover the timeless principles that set them on the path to financial success. I think the people they studied are good examples of how I believe, and I suggest you read this book.

I. **Live Below Your Means:**

- Millionaires aren't always about flashy living. They understand the art of spending less than they earn.
- Living below your means is not about deprivation; it's a strategic choice to prioritize saving and investing over unnecessary extravagances.

II. **Avoid Debt:**

- Debt can be a tricky slope. Millionaires are cautious about it, especially for non-essential items.

- By minimizing debt, they reduce financial risk and avoid paying unnecessary interest, letting their wealth grow efficiently.

III. **Invest Wisely:**

- Forget about risky bets. Millionaires focus on smart, long-term investments.
- They create a balanced portfolio, including stocks, bonds, and real estate, aligning with their risk tolerance and financial goals.

IV. **Live in a Modest Home:**

- Ever wonder why millionaires' homes often seem ordinary? It's because they choose practicality over extravagance.
- Living in a modest home aligns with their financial values, allowing them to channel resources into wealth-building rather than high housing costs.

V. **Be Financially Independent:**

- Financial independence isn't just a goal; it's a lifestyle for millionaires.
- It means having enough savings and investments to cover living expenses without relying on external sources of income.

VI. **Avoid Buying Status Symbols:**

- Millionaires don't fall for the trap of flashy status symbols like luxury cars or extravagant jewelry.
- Their frugality contributes to wise saving and investing decisions, steering clear of societal pressures for conspicuous consumption.

VII. **Be Frugal buying vehicles:**

- Forget about the allure of luxury cars. Millionaires are practical when it comes to transportation.
- They opt for reliable, cost-effective vehicles, understanding that a car is a means of transportation, not a status symbol.

Chapter 3: Navigating Your Financial Terrain for Success

Understanding Your Financial Landscape

Understanding your financial landscape is the first step towards financial success. This chapter will guide you through assessing your current finances and setting realistic goals, ensuring you're equipped to make informed decisions.

A. Assessing Current Finances

1. **Creating a Comprehensive Budget**
   - Your budget is your financial compass. Start by listing all your income sources and categorizing your expenses. Use tools and apps to streamline the process and gain a clear snapshot of where your money is going.
2. **Analyzing Income and Expenses**
   - Track your spending habits diligently. Analyze your income against your expenditures. Identify patterns and areas where you can cut back.
3. **Identifying Discretionary and Non-Discretionary Spending**
   - Recognize essential expenses (non-discretionary) versus non-essential ones

(discretionary). This clarity will be pivotal in making conscious choices about your spending.

B. Setting Realistic Financial Goals

1. **Short-Term vs. Long-Term Goals**
    - Short-term goals provide quick wins, boosting motivation.
    - Long-term goals create a vision for your financial future.
2. **Prioritizing Goals Based on Urgency and Importance**[2]
    - Apply the Eisenhower Matrix to categorize goals: urgent and important, important but not urgent, urgent but not important, neither urgent nor important. This helps prioritize effectively.
3. **Creating a Roadmap for Financial Success**
    - Develop a step-by-step plan to achieve your goals. Break down larger objectives into manageable tasks.
    - Regularly revisit and adjust your roadmap as circumstances change.

Navigating Your Financial Landscape: A Practical Guide

Navigating your financial landscape is akin to setting sail on uncharted waters. Assessing your current position and plotting a course are crucial steps toward reaching your financial destination.

A. Assessing Current Finances

1. **Creating a Comprehensive Budget**
    - Your budget is your financial GPS. It not only tells you where your money is going but also helps you chart a course toward your financial goals.
    - Tools like budgeting apps can automate this process, making it easier to track and manage your finances.
2. **Analyzing Income and Expenses**
    - Dive deep into your financial data. Analyze your income sources and ensure they align with your goals. Identify areas where you can optimize and cut unnecessary expenses.
3. **Identifying Discretionary and Non-Discretionary Spending**
    - Knowing the difference between essential and non-essential expenses is crucial. It

allows you to make informed decisions when prioritizing your spending.

- Non-discretionary spending includes necessities like housing, utilities, and groceries. Discretionary spending covers non-essential items or services that enhance your lifestyle but aren't fundamental to survival. Some non-discretionary spending can still be honed in cutting back on the degree of spending in those areas.

B. Setting Realistic Financial Goals

1. **Short-Term vs. Long-Term Goals**
   - Setting short-term goals creates a series of achievable milestones. These small victories build momentum, propelling you toward more significant accomplishments.
   - Long-term goals provide a roadmap for your financial journey. They give you a sense of purpose and direction, guiding your day-to-day decisions.

2. **Prioritizing Goals Based on Urgency and Importance**
    - The Eisenhower Matrix, a tool often used in business, is equally effective for personal finance. Categorize your goals based on urgency and importance to prioritize your focus and energy.
    - Urgent and important goals demand immediate attention, while important but not urgent goals require strategic planning. Evaluate what truly matters in your financial landscape.
3. **Creating a Roadmap for Financial Success**
    - Your financial roadmap is your action plan. Break down larger goals into manageable tasks, making the journey less overwhelming.
    - Be flexible. Life is unpredictable, and your roadmap should adapt to changes in income, expenses, and external factors.

By understanding your current financial situation and setting realistic goals, you've equipped yourself with the tools necessary for financial success. This chapter serves as your compass, guiding you through the intricate terrain of personal finance. As you continue this journey, remember that navigating your financial landscape is a dynamic process. Regular reassessment and adjustments will ensure you stay on course towards a prosperous future.

Chapter 4: Mastering Your Money with Budgeting Wisdom Budgeting Fundamentals

Budgeting is the backbone of financial success. In this chapter, we will unravel the secrets behind creating a realistic budget and the art of tracking and monitoring your spending.

A. Creating a Realistic Budget

1. **Making a List of Needs and Wants**
    - I know I keep mentioning this but it is very important. Distinguish between needs and wants to prioritize spending. Write a list and keep going over it to see if you can make more adjustments. Have a critical eye on the needs to see if they are truly needs.
2. **Identifying Areas for Potential Savings**
    - Scrutinize your spending to find areas for potential savings.
    - Consider negotiating bills, opting for generic brands, or exploring alternative, cost-effective solutions.

3. **Setting Aside Money for Emergencies and Savings**
    - Prioritize setting aside money for emergencies and savings before allocating funds to discretionary spending.
    - Emergency funds act as a financial safety net, providing peace of mind in unpredictable times.
    - If helping children further their education, start a saving for that now.

B. Tracking and Monitoring Spending

1. **Divide Money into Envelopes and Only Spend What You Have Planned For**
    - Embrace the envelope system: allocate cash for different spending categories.
    - When the envelope is empty, you're done spending in that category until the next budgeting period.
2. **Utilizing Budgeting Apps and Tools**
    - Leverage technology with budgeting apps tailored to your needs.
    - Apps automate tracking, providing real-time insights into your spending habits.

- Pay your bills on auto-pay. This ensures they are paid on time.

3. **Establishing a Routine for Tracking Expenses**
    - Consistency is key. Set aside specific times each week to review and categorize your expenses.
    - Make tracking expenses a habit, ensuring you stay informed about your financial landscape.
4. **Making Adjustments Based on Spending Patterns**
    - Regularly evaluate your spending patterns.
    - Adjust your budget to reflect changes in income, expenses, or financial goals.

Budgeting is the cornerstone of financial empowerment. By creating a realistic budget and mastering the art of tracking and monitoring spending, you gain control over your financial destiny. Remember, as you navigate this journey, consistency and adaptability are your allies. Budgeting isn't a rigid framework but a dynamic tool that evolves with your financial landscape.

Chapter 5: Entertainment: Debunking the Myth that Fun Costs Money

In a world where the allure of expensive entertainment is prevalent, let's shatter the myth that having a good time requires breaking the bank. This chapter explores the vast realm of free and low-cost entertainment, emphasizing the significance of family time and shared experiences.

A. Fun Doesn't Have to Break the Bank

- **Challenge the Status Quo:** Reassure readers that fun isn't synonymous with spending money. The most memorable moments often come from shared experiences rather than pricey outings.
- **Redefine Entertainment:** Encourage a mindset shift from consumer-driven entertainment to the wealth of joy found in simple, cost-effective activities.

B. Unearthing Free and Low-Cost Entertainment Options

- **Libraries: A Hidden Treasure**
    - Libraries offer a treasure trove of free entertainment. From books and audiobooks to movies and educational programs, libraries cater to a myriad of interests.

- **Parks and Outdoor Adventures**
    - Explore the great outdoors without spending a dime. Parks provide a natural backdrop for family picnics, hikes, and playtime.
- **Community Events: The Heartbeat of Togetherness**
    - Keep an eye on local community events. Festivals, fairs, and gatherings offer entertainment without straining your wallet.
- **DIY Crafts: Creative Adventures at Home**
    - Embrace the art of Do-It-Yourself crafts. Engage in family projects that not only provide entertainment but also foster creativity and collaboration.
- **Digital Alternatives: The Libby App and Beyond**
    - Introduce digital alternatives to expensive subscriptions. The Libby app, for instance, opens a gateway to a vast collection of books, audiobooks, and magazines without any cost.

C. Emphasizing the Importance of Family Time and Shared Experiences

- **Quality Over Quantity**
    - Highlight the research-backed notion that shared experiences contribute significantly to family bonds and overall happiness.
- **Making Memories Last**
    - Advocate for the value of memories over material possessions. A day at the park or a DIY craft project can create lasting impressions.
- **Creating Family Traditions**
    - Encourage the development of family traditions that don't hinge on spending money. Whether it's a weekly game night or a monthly outdoor adventure, these traditions become cherished moments.

D. Subscription Audit: Trim the Excess

- **Identify Subscriptions:** List your subscriptions, from streaming services to magazines and beyond. Can you eliminate some or all of them?

- **Evaluate Necessity:** Challenge the necessity of each subscription. Are they enhancing your life or draining your finances?
- **Find Alternatives:** Look at alternatives to paid subscriptions.

E. Ditch TV and Movies Subscriptions

There are several platforms where you can watch TV shows and movies for free, supported by ads. Here are some alternatives to cable:

Tubi TV is a popular ad-supported streaming service with a broad range of movies and TV shows.

Crackle is a free streaming service offering a variety of movies and TV shows. It is owned by Sony Pictures Entertainment.

Pluto TV is a free, ad-supported streaming service that offers a wide range of live TV channels and on-demand content.

IMDb TV is owned by Amazon, it provides a selection of movies and TV shows for free with occasional advertisements.

Vudu offers a selection of ad-supported movies and TV shows that you can watch for free.

Peacock Free, by NBC Universal, has a free tier that provides access to a limited library of movies, TV shows, and exclusive content.

Kanopy is a streaming service that partners with public libraries and universities. If your library is connected, you can access a range of movies and documentaries for free.

Popcornflix offers a variety of movies and TV shows for free with ads. It covers different genres, including drama, comedy, horror, and more.

Crunchyroll, if you enjoy anime, Crunchyroll provides a free, ad-supported tier with a selection of anime series.

YouTube offers a growing collection of movies and TV shows for free.

Redbox Free Live TV offers a free, ad-supported streaming service with a mix of live TV channels and on-demand content.

XUMO provides free live and on-demand streaming channels across various genres.

Remember that the availability of content may vary based on your location, and these services often rotate their content libraries. Additionally, these platforms are ad-supported, so you'll encounter occasional advertisements during your viewing experience.

Entertainment on a Budget: Crafting Moments, Not Bills

In this chapter, we've dismantled the notion that fun comes with a hefty price tag. By exploring free and low-cost entertainment options, emphasizing the importance of family time, and auditing subscriptions, we've paved the way for a more fulfilling and budget-friendly approach to leisure. The journey to financial freedom doesn't mean sacrificing joy; instead, it's about discovering the abundance of delight that exists in the everyday moments shared with loved ones.

Chapter 6: Fortifying Your Financial Fortress

In the unpredictable dance of life, financial resilience is your partner, ensuring you stay on your feet even when the music gets chaotic. This chapter dives into creating a robust safety net and exploring avenues to bolster your income streams.

A. Emergency Fund and Financial Safety Nets

1. **Establishing and Maintaining an Emergency Fund**
    - An emergency fund is your financial shield against unexpected storms. Aim for at least three to six months' worth of living expenses tucked away.
2. **Creating a Plan for Unexpected Financial Challenges**
    - Anticipate the unexpected by crafting a financial contingency plan.
    - Outline steps to navigate unforeseen challenges, ensuring you're prepared for whatever financial curveballs life throws your way.
    - Figure out how much you want to allocate for gifts throughout the year. Divide that yearly amount by the paychecks you have

each year. Save that amount each paycheck so you don't feel overwhelmed when it comes time to purchase gifts. Watch for sales during the year and buy what you need for further savings.

B. Increasing Income Streams

1. **Exploring Part-Time Employment Opportunities**
    - Part-time jobs offer additional income without the commitment of a full-time position.
    - Seek opportunities aligned with your skills and schedule to maximize earnings.
    - There are many remote opportunities to look into that you may not have thought of before.
2. **Investing in Education and Skill Development**
    - Continuous learning is an investment in your earning potential.
    - I am a big fan of always learning something new. There are so many opportunities to learn things that did not exist twenty years ago.

- Explore online courses and workshops to enhance your skills and make yourself more marketable. Many jobs that exist today didn't exist ten years ago. Keep honing your skills to remain marketable.

- One place I have taken free classes is on the Alison website.[3]

3. **Leveraging Side Hustles and Freelance Work**
    - Side hustles can be lucrative and provide flexibility.
    - Identify your skills or passions and explore freelance opportunities that align with them.
    - Even though I didn't work full time after I had my first baby. I did do several things on the side. I did custodial jobs, piecework sewing, placed exchange students, Co-op food orders, and babysitting.
4. **Reselling Items You No Longer Want or Need**
    - Declutter your space while making extra cash by selling items you no longer need.

- Online platforms provide easy avenues for reselling.

5. **Barter, Trade for Goods, or Services**
    - Embrace the age-old practice of bartering. Exchange goods or services with others, creating a win-win situation.
6. **Negotiate Lower Prices for Services**
    - Negotiate with service providers, from the Internet to all types of insurance.
    - Research competitor prices and use that information as leverage for negotiation.
7. **Extra Payments on Loans: A Long-Term Savings Strategy**
    - Paying extra on loans, whether it's your mortgage, car payment or credit cards, can significantly reduce interest payments over time.
    - This is a long-term strategy that pays off by saving you money in the grand financial scheme.
    - For instance, consider a $400,000 mortgage with a 30-year term and a fixed interest rate of 7%. If you pay an extra $100 per month

towards the principal, you could potentially save over $73,000 in interest payments and shorten the loan term by more than three years.[4]

- If you have a credit card balance with 18% interest and pay $200/month, without adding to it, it will take 5 years and 2 months to pay off the balance. The total interest is $4,308.61
- If instead, you put $200 in the bank and added $200 each month (2.4% interest), in the 5 years and 2 months you would have $13,178[5]
- Was what you spent $8000 on five years ago worth the $5,178 difference?

8. **Buy Used Items: A Frugal Lifestyle Choice**
    - Opt for used items. Anything from vehicles, clothing, books, basically look to see if there is something you are looking to buy that you can buy used that is still in good shape. In looking, check out refurbished items. Make a game out of hunting for bargains.

- Ensure the used item is still in good condition and can be maintained without excessive costs.

9. **Explore Higher CD Rates at Your Bank**
    - Investigate Certificate of Deposit (CD) rates at your bank.
    - CDs often offer higher interest rates than regular savings accounts, providing a safe way to earn a bit more on your savings.
10. **Free Money**
    - Don't leave money on the table. Take advantage if your employer offers a match towards your retirement plan.

A Resilient Financial Future Awaits

In the symphony of financial life, resilience is your melody. By establishing a robust emergency fund, exploring diverse income streams, and adopting frugal yet strategic financial practices, you fortify your financial fortress. As you embrace the art of financial resilience, remember the words of wisdom: "Small changes, when done consistently, lead to significant outcomes." Your journey to financial resilience is a series of these small, impactful steps.

Chapter 7: Thriving Together - Building Stronger Family Bonds

In the tapestry of financial well-being, family forms the intricate threads that weave a story of shared prosperity. This chapter unveils the keys to fostering open communication about finances and imparting the invaluable gift of financial literacy to the younger generation.

A. Open Communication about Finances

1. **Fostering a Transparent and Collaborative Financial Environment**
    - Transparency is the cornerstone of a financially healthy family. Encourage open conversations about money matters, creating an environment where everyone feels heard and understood.
2. **Involving Family Members in Financial Decisions**
    - Financial decisions impact the whole family. Involve each member in discussions about budgets, goals, and major financial choices. A collective effort strengthens the family's financial foundation.

3. **Celebrating Financial Milestones and Successes**
    - Recognize and celebrate financial milestones, whether big or small. It could be paying off a debt, reaching a savings goal, or achieving a significant financial milestone. Celebrations create a positive atmosphere and reinforce shared accomplishments.

B. Teaching Financial Literacy to Children

1. **Introducing Age-Appropriate Financial Concepts**
    - Begin teaching financial literacy early. Introduce basic concepts like saving, spending, and budgeting in a way that aligns with a child's age and comprehension level.
2. **Encouraging Responsible Money Habits from a Young Age**
    - Foster responsible money habits by encouraging children to save a portion of their allowance or earnings.
    - Teach them the value of delayed gratification and the importance of careful spending.

3. **Instilling a Sense of Financial Responsibility in Children**
    - Instill a sense of responsibility by involving children in decisions related to their finances.
    - As they grow older, gradually introduce more complex financial concepts, preparing them for a future of financial independence.

Thriving Together: A Symphony of Financial Harmony

In the rhythm of family life, financial harmony is the melody that resonates through generations. By fostering open communication and imparting financial literacy, families can not only weather financial storms but also thrive together. Remember, the family unit is not just a sum of individuals; it's a collective force capable of achieving financial success and building a legacy of prosperity.

Chapter 8: Mastering Practical Money-Saving Strategies

A. Smart Shopping Techniques

1. **Watch for Sales, Buy Extra, Stock Up for Future Savings**
    - Capitalizing on sales by stocking up during promotions prevents future expenses when prices rise. I love after-holiday sales. Many things are on sale that are not specifically for holidays.
2. **Comparing Prices and Exploring Alternative Products**
    - Don't settle for the first option. Compare prices and explore alternative products that offer similar functionality at a lower cost.
3. **Avoid Shopping Companions Who Tend to Add Things to Your Cart**
    - Beware of who joins you on shopping trips to avoid unnecessary purchases influenced by others.
4. **Utilize Cashback Apps for Extra Savings**
    - Leverage cashback apps like Upside, Ibotta, and Rakuten.

B. Savvy Financial Decisions Beyond the Store

- **Evaluate Solar Options with a Critical Eye**
    - Calculate the potential savings before investing in solar. Where we live with the prices we were quoted, we would never break even. But, we did find a local electrician who could install the same system for just under half the price. With an option like this, we would have to pay cash.

  Know Your Prices
    - Develop a keen awareness of standard prices for items you regularly purchase to identify genuine discounts.
- **Explore Diverse Purchase Avenues:**
    - Look at online stores, wholesale stores, thrift stores, dollar stores, clearance sections, overstock stores, Facebook groups, eBay, and yard sales.
    - Help organize a community swap event where people bring their unused items and anyone can help themselves to what they can use.

- **Strategic Cart Management for Online Shopping**
    - If I see something I want on Amazon, I put it in my cart, and then click save for later. When it goes on sale, I buy it if I still need it.

C. Meal Planning and Smart Grocery Shopping

1. **Create Budget-Friendly Meal Plans**
    - Plan meals based on what you have on hand and what is on sale to maximize savings.
2. **Plan Your Trips to Do as Many Things as Possible**
    - Combine errands to save time and gas.

Chapter 9: Everyday Money-Saving Wisdom

Welcome to the heart of practical money-saving wisdom, where frugality meets efficiency, and every dollar is a soldier in your financial army. I'll share some nuggets of financial insight that have served me well over the years.

Food: Fuel for the Body and Budget

- **Avoid Shopping Hungry to Dodge Impulse Buys**
    - Shopping on an empty stomach often leads to unnecessary purchases. Eat before you shop for a clear-headed approach.
- **Always Have a Snack On the Go**
    - Whether it's a day out or heading to work, carrying a homemade lunch or snack can save you from the temptation of fast food. Don't forget a water bottle.
    - Make some easy-to-grab foods that can be eaten on the way out the door. Such as breakfast burritos, bean burritos, peanut butter and jelly sandwiches, and muffins.

These things can be frozen for a quick easy meal.

- **Buy in Bulk and Embrace Storage Hacks**
    - Purchase in bulk for significant savings. I raised my family with most of our groceries coming in 25# or 50# bags. I would store large amounts of bulk food in plastic buckets, often available from store bakeries.
    - Buy what is on sale and buy extra, eventually you will have a good amount stored. Do compare prices between stores, just because it is on sale at one store, it might be cheaper at another. When you do this, eventually you will have everything you need on hand to help avoid extra runs to the store.
    - During the pandemic shutdown, there was nothing I needed. I went two months before going to a store and then it was to get fresh produce. I had plenty of toilet

paper that I had stocked up on years earlier. I didn't like hoard shaming, if I had not bought things years earlier, I would have been buying what others needed then.

- **Master the Art of Meal Planning**
    - Plan meals based on what you have on hand and what is on sale. This strategic approach minimizes waste and maximizes savings.
- **Cooking at Home: A Financial Superpower**
    - Cooking from scratch not only saves money but also enhances your culinary skills. Start small, and gradually incorporate more homemade meals.
    - Have food prepared that is available to be eaten when someone is hungry. For example, I normally have things like baked potatoes in the refrigerator.

- **Freeze Like a Pro**
    - Utilize your freezer for batch cooking and preserving ingredients. I figured if something came on a frozen pizza, I could freeze it. So, when I had my eight children at home, I would buy a #10 can of sliced olives, drain it, freeze it on a cookie sheet, and then when frozen, I would package it up in plastic bags. I did this with pineapple, peppers, onions, grated cheese, as well as other things.
    - When batch cooking, freeze whole meals and portion sizes as needed, for quick and convenient options.
    - Make freezer meals by putting all the ingredients in a bag that you can put in a crockpot or Instant Pot for easy meal preparation on busy days.
- **Vacuum sealer**
    - Extend the life of foods by vacuum sealing whether it is something in the freezer,

refrigerator, or pantry. I like to vacuum-seal nuts in jars.

- **Baking: A Therapeutic and Budget-Friendly Activity**
    - Making bread, pizza crusts, pasta, and more not only provides tasty results but also cuts down on expenses. Get the family involved for more fun.

Gardening and DIY: Where Savings and Self-Sufficiency Meet

- **Explore Gardening, Even in Small Spaces**
    - Gardening, whether in a backyard or through container gardening, offers fresh produce at a fraction of the cost. Fresh homegrown vegetables taste so much better too.
- **Sprouting and Microgreens for Healthy Choices**
    - Sprouting and growing microgreens at home provide a cost-effective way to add healthy greens to your diet.

- **Dehydrating: Preserve the Harvest**
    - Dehydrating fruits and vegetables is an excellent way to extend the shelf life of your produce. If you have backpackers in your family you can dehydrate other foods like frozen vegetables or cooked soup to easily reconstitute on the trip.
    - In the fall, we often have three large dehydrators going at one time. My husband does the apples, I do everything else.
- **Reuse and Repurpose:**
    - I wash and reuse many of the zip-lock bags I use, even though my husband doesn't like me doing that.
    - Make bone broth from bones, and vegetable broth from vegetable scraps. Freeze in portion sizes.

Beauty and Personal Care: DIY Style

- **Cut Costs with DIY Haircuts and Grooming**

    - Learn to cut hair, and do manicures, and pedicures at home. Online tutorials, especially on YouTube, can guide you through the process. Many people did this during the pandemic shutdown. This idea is not new to me. I am sixty-four and I have never been to a beauty salon. I have always cut my hair and given myself permanent. My mother did until I left home. Most of my children do the same.

- **Financially Savvy Choices: Phone Plans and Utilities**

    - Opt for phone plans that cost under $20 per month, many in our family use Mint Mobile. We get talk, text, and data for $15/month. You do need to pay quarterly or yearly though. Some other companies have plans for $20 or less a month.

    - Explore alternatives to traditional trash services. Where we live we can take our trash directly to the waste transfer station. This saves us about $35/month.

- If you are trying to save on utilities, there are a few things you can do. Obviously, change the thermostat to use less. One thing you should do is check to see if you have adequate insulation. Interestingly, when we added more insulation to our attic, it was cheaper to have someone come to do it.
- My husband is an engineer. Years ago we had a salesman try to sell us a product to reflect heat. My husband made a box with lights, thermometers, and insulation then did some testing. He found that heavy-duty aluminum foil worked just as well. We bought a case of Mylar blankets. We had a son go up in the attic and lay them over the insulation. It made more than a ten-degree difference.
- If you haven't already, change your light bulbs to LED bulbs.
- Watch YouTube videos to see if you can do minor maintenance or car repairs yourself.

Unexpected Savings Opportunities

- **Direct Casket Purchase: Funeral Planning**
    - Plan for the unexpected by knowing you can buy caskets directly from manufacturers or retailers like Costco, often at about 1/3 of the cost. Caskets are mailed directly to your mortuary, usually in three days or less.
- **Coupon Philosophy: Practical Savings**
    - Use coupons wisely. If it's something you're already buying, embrace the savings. However, be discerning, as sometimes coupon deals may not be the most cost-effective. I rarely use coupons for food unless it is for a specific ingredient. I do like coupons for eating out. At my local grocery store, they have an app where I can click on coupons they offer. Otherwise, I found it not worth the time.

- **Wind and Solar Power: Hang Your Laundry**
    - Harness wind and solar power in a simple way—hang your laundry to dry. It's eco-friendly and budget-friendly.

Savings Beyond the Plate: Dining Out, Crafting, and DIY Magic

Eating at restaurants can be a delightful experience, but the bill can quickly escalate, especially with beverages. Here are some tips to savor both the flavors and your savings:

- **Opt for Water to Slash Dining Costs**
    - Choosing water over pricier beverages at restaurants can significantly reduce your overall bill.
- **Less Dining Out, More Copycat Cooking**
    - Cutting back on restaurant visits and experimenting with copycat recipes at home not only saves money but also allows you to enjoy your favorite dishes on a budget.

And now, let's dive into the world of creativity and resourcefulness, where DIY solutions become the keys to affordability:

- **Crafting Cost-Effective Alternatives**
    - Crafting offers a fantastic way to bring your ideas to life without breaking the bank. From home decor to personalized gifts, the possibilities are endless.
- **Sewing: A Stitch in Time Saves More Than Nine**
    - While sewing can be a cost-effective way to create unique items, it's essential to weigh the costs of making versus buying, ensuring you're maximizing savings. The cost of sewing seems to go in cycles. Sometimes it is a money-saving thing, other times, it is cheaper to buy things ready-made. It is good to know how to mend and alter things.
- **DIY: Beauty on a Budget**
    - Beauty products can be pricey, but with a bit of research and creativity, you can craft

your own. I see a product advertised and know I cannot afford it. So, I do some research by looking at what the ingredients are and make my own moisturizers and mineral makeup at a fraction of the cost. Online platforms like eBay offer the necessary materials.

- **Laundry Soap DIY: (No) Suds Without the Splurge**
  - Making your laundry soap is not only straightforward but also budget-friendly. Equal parts of powdered Borax, washing soda, and grated soap (Fels Naptha, Kirks, Zote, or Ivory Soap) make for an effective, economical solution. Use 1-3 tablespoons per load. I have made this but don't always use it.
- **Cleaning Supplies Reimagined**
  - Everyday cleaning supplies can be replaced with budget-friendly alternatives like vinegar, baking soda, and rubbing alcohol.

These common household items work wonders without the hefty price tag.

- **DIY Dog Treats: Tail-Wagging Savings**
    - Extend your money-saving prowess to your pets. Making dog treats at home ensures your pet enjoys tasty snacks without denting your wallet.

DIY Celebrations: More Heart, Less Spending

- **Personal Touches for Special Events like Birthdays and Weddings**
    - Create memorable celebrations without breaking the bank by organizing DIY events. From decorations to food, the possibilities are endless. Get your friends to help. Have fun!

In our journey to financial mastery, these practical tips can be the wind beneath your financial wings. Remember, every small change adds up, and before you know it, you'll be navigating the seas of financial freedom with confidence.

Chapter 10: Thrifty and Healthy: Building a Budget-Friendly Food Storage

In the world of budget-friendly food storage, I've shared valuable lessons with countless individuals on how to strengthen their pantry without breaking the bank. Today, I'll guide you through practical steps to achieve this, starting with a humble yet versatile ingredient – oatmeal.

Oatmeal: The Budget-Friendly Superfood

- **Buying in Bulk:**
    - Consider purchasing a 25-pound bag of oatmeal if available or explore grocery stores with bulk bins.
    - Bulk buying often provides cost savings compared to smaller packages.
- **Cereal Replacement:**
    - Swap expensive cereals for budget-friendly oatmeal or other grains, to save money on your grocery bill. Figure out what an ounce of cooked oatmeal cost you and compare it to an ounce of purchased cereal.

    - Oatmeal is not only economical but also a nutritious alternative.

- **Gluten-Free Option:**
    - For those with gluten sensitivity, replace wheat flour with oat flour. Oats are gluten free but often produced in factories that also produce gluten products. Packages will tell you if they were produced in a gluten free environment.
    - Easily make oat flour by blending oatmeal in a blender.

- **The Versatility of Oats:**
    - Utilize oatmeal in various recipes, including bread, cookies, pancakes, waffles, muffins, granola, energy balls, and homemade plant-based milk.

Affordable Protein: Beans

- **Cost-Effective Protein Source:**
    - Replace expensive meats with budget-friendly beans.

    - Consider buying dry beans in larger quantities for even more savings. Dry beans are more economical, but canned beans offer convenience.
- **Varieties to Start With:**
    - Pinto, black, garbanzo (chick peas), red, lima, and white beans are versatile options to start with. There are dozens of other varieties.

Staples for Every Pantry: Rice and Quinoa

- **Affordable Grains:**
    - Add rice and quinoa to your pantry for versatile meal options. Quinoa is a complete protein.

1. **Quinoa Salad:**
    - Toss quinoa with colorful vegetables and a light dressing for a nutritious salad.

2. **Fried Rice:**

    - Combine cooked rice with vegetables, soy sauce, and a protein source for a quick and affordable meal.

1. **Beans and Rice:**

    - I enjoy rice, beans, and salsa. Such a quick and tasty meal.

Homemade Bread and Beyond

- **Venture into Bread Making:**

    - Beyond traditional loaves of bread, explore making pizza crusts, biscuits, pancakes, and tortillas at home.

Health Benefits of Budget-Friendly Eating

- **Nutritional Value:**

    - This budget-friendly approach isn't just about saving money; it's about enhancing your health.

- Oats, beans, rice, and quinoa are nutrient-rich, providing essential vitamins and minerals. After using these types of foods, add more whole foods to your menu.

In adopting these practices, not only will your grocery bills shrink, but your health will flourish. Embrace the simplicity of oatmeal, the affordability of beans, and the versatility of grains, all while enjoying the wholesome journey to budget-friendly and healthy living.

Note: The information provided are inspired by general knowledge of budget-friendly and healthy eating practices. For more detailed nutritional information, it is recommended to consult with a nutritionist or healthcare professional.

Chapter 11: Savings on a Plate: Frugalicious Feasts for the Budget-Savvy Gourmet

I am going to give you some simple recipes for you to try. I will include in the list of resources, some of my favorite cookbooks that use whole foods. You do not need to buy these books, the authors all have YouTube channels where they show you how to make hundreds of recipes and most of them have blog pages as well. I just want to spark some ideas.

Oatmeal Banana Cookies

1 cup oatmeal

1 very ripe banana, mashed

Stir then add any of the options. Divide and roll into about 8 balls.

Bake at 350°

Optional, add 1/2 cup chocolate chips, dried fruit, flaked coconut or nuts

Place onto baking sheet, press to flatten the balls of dough. Cookies will not spread much during baking, Bake for about 15 minutes or until cookies are lightly brown and set. If you use old fashioned oats, they will take longer to bake and will be a bit chewier. If that is not what you want, take those oats and pulse them in a food processor first to break them up a bit. Store in the refrigerator.

Oatmeal Energy Balls

3 cups quick oats

1 cup peanut butter

1/2 cup honey

1/2 cup of whatever you want to add, chocolate chips, nuts or dried fruit

Mix together, roll in balls and refrigerate

Homemade Oat Milk

Blend: 1 part oats with 4 parts water for 15 to 30 seconds, don't do too long or it will become slimy. Strain through a cheesecloth-type fabric, and sweeten to taste. You might want to add a pinch of salt.

To help with texture, soak the oatmeal for fifteen minutes in water first. Drain that water and add new water when blending.

Three Bean Chili

Sauté 1 diced onion with 2 Tbs. garlic

Add:

2 cups water

2 Tbs. chili powder

1 tsp. cumin

6 oz. tomato paste (or 2 8oz. cans of tomato sauce)

3 cans of a variety of beans (1 1/2 Cup each) (pinto, black, kidney, red, white, lima, or garbanzo beans)

Simmer until warm. Can add some corn.

Bean Burgers:

1 1/5 cups drained beans

1/2 tsp. cumin

1/2 tsp. smoked paprika

1 tsp. garlic powder

1 tsp. onion powder

1/4 cup oatmeal.

1 Tablespoon ground flax seeds, set in 3 Tbs. water for a few minutes (or 1 egg)

Form into patties and bake at 375 for 1/2 hour.

This is just a basic idea. There are a lot of recipes available to try. Adjust and use the seasonings you like.

Simple Hummus

Blend:

1-1/2 cups cooked garbanzo beans

1 clove garlic

2 Tbsps. lemon juice

1 tbsp. Tahini (optional)

1/2 tsp. salt

Chocolate Hummus

Blend:

1-1/2 cups cooked garbanzo beans

1 tbsp. peanut butter

1/2 tsp. salt

4 Tbsp. cocoa powder

1/4 Cup sweetener of choice

1/2 tsp vanilla

White Bean Mayonnaise/Dressing Replacement

Blend until creamy:

1 1/2 cups drained cooked white beans

2 Tbs. lemon juice

2 Tbs. onion

1 tsp. garlic powder

1 tsp. onion powder

1 Tbs. white wine or apple cider vinegar

1/2 tsp. salt

1/4 tsp. dry mustard

Can use as a base for creamy dressings.

This is better if replacing some of the beans with raw cashews. They need to be pre-soaked or used in a high speed blender.

Cheese Replacement or Sauce

Use the white bean mayonnaise recipe and add 3-4 Tbs. tapioca flour, add 1/4 cup nutritional yeast if you have some, blend then cook for a few minutes until thickened. Dilute a bit when using as a sauce.

Use in macaroni and cheese, as a pizza topping, or in lasagna.

Garbanzo Bean Gravy

My favorite gravy recipe. To me it tastes just like the gravy I make from turkey drippings.

1 1/2 cups (15 oz. can) garbanzo beans

1/3 cup Nutritional Yeast

1/4 cups chopped onion

1 teas. Salt

2 Tbs. Soy sauce

1/4 tsp. Pepper

1 Tbs. Garlic

1 tsp Dried Sage

1-1/2 to 2 cups hot boiled water

1/2 tsp. Kitchen Bouquet (optional)

Change it up with other herbs

Put all of the ingredients into a blender that can handle hot water (otherwise use warm or cold water and cook after it is blended) and blend until smooth (about 1 minute).

3-Minute Bean Flour Soups[6]

Cream soups made from bean flours cook in only 3 minutes! Four tablespoons white bean flour and 2 teaspoons bouillon combine to make a creamy substitute equal to a whole can of store-bought cream soup.

Whisk bean flour into soup stock, or use hot water flavored with bouillon.

Cook and stir 3 for minutes. Blend after cooking, if desired, for a creamier soup.

For pea and lentil soups, use 1-3 T. flour per cup of liquid depending on how thick you want it.

I learned about this from Rita Bingham's book "Country Beans - How to cook dry beans in only 3 minutes!"

***To make bean flour, use a grain grinder, coffee grinder, or blender. If the flour is not fine, cook it anyway, it will take longer. Then you will want to blend the mixture, either during the cooking time or after.

5-Minute Refried Bean Dip Mix

(Also from Rita Bingham)

3 c. pinto or black bean flour	1 T. salt
1 t. cumin 1 T. chili powder	1/4 t. garlic powder
	2 t. instant minced onions (opt.)

Mix and store in airtight container. Store up to one month on the shelf, indefinitely if refrigerated.

To prepare, whisk... 3/4 c. of mixture into 2 1/2 c. boiling water.

Cook, while stirring, over medium heat for about 1 minute, until mixture thickens. Reduce heat to low. Cover pan and cook 4 minutes.

Add 1/2 c. Picante sauce (or to taste). Mixture thickens as it cools and will stay thick even after reheating. Use for burritos or dip.

Depression Era Dump Cake

1 ½ cups of flour

1 cup of granulated sugar

1 tsp. baking soda

1 tsp. baking powder

1/4 cup cocoa powder

1/4 tsp. salt

1 tsp. vanilla extract

1 Tbs. vinegar

5 Tbs. oil (applesauce or mashed beans)

1 cup of lukewarm water

Preheat the oven to 350 degrees F (175 degrees C).

Put all the dry ingredients into an ungreased 8" cake pan and stir.

Make an indention in the middle and add the wet ingredients. Stir until the batter is smooth. Bake for about 30 minutes, until done. To use beans in the recipe mash them well or put them in a food processor with just a little bit of water.

Taco Seasoning

1/2 cup chili powder

1/4 cup onion powder

1 tablespoon garlic powder

1/8 cup ground cumin

1 tablespoon paprika

1 tablespoon sea salt

Dry Onion Soup Mix

2/3 cup dried, minced onion

3 teaspoons parsley flakes

1 Tbs. onion powder

2 teaspoons turmeric

4 Tbs. mix equals 1 packet

1 teaspoon celery salt

1 teaspoon sea salt

1 teaspoon sugar

1/2 teaspoon ground pepper

Chili Seasoning Mix

4 Tbsp. chili powder

2 Tbsp. ground cumin

1 tsp cayenne pepper

1 Tbsp. garlic powder

1 Tbsp. onion powder

2 Tbsp. oregano

4 tsp salt

1 tsp pepper

Ranch Dressing Mix

2 Tbsp. onion flakes

2 Tbsp. dried parsley

1 tsp dried dill

1 tsp garlic powder

1 tsp onion powder

1/2 tsp dried basil

1/2 tsp pepper

Pumpkin Pie Spice Mix

2 tsp ground cinnamon

¼ tsp ground nutmeg

¼ tsp ground ginger

1/8 tsp ground cloves

Apple Pie Spice Mix

3 Tbsp. ground cinnamon

½ Tbsp. allspice

1 tsp nutmeg

1 tsp ginger

Master Mix Recipe (Like Bisquick)

(makes 9 cups of mix)

8 cups flour (can use a combination of white, whole wheat, and oats-blend oatmeal in a blender)

1 1/3 cups nonfat dry milk

4 tablespoons baking powder

1 teaspoon salt

Drop Biscuits (makes 10 biscuits)

2 cups Master Mix

¾ cups water

¼ cup vegetable oil

Stir just until ingredients are wet.

Divide dough into 10 parts, drop 4 inches apart on baking sheet. Press to flatten

Bake 10 - 12 minutes until lightly browned. At 400 degrees

Pancakes (makes about 12 medium sized pancakes)

2 cups Master Mix	2 eggs, beaten
1 cup water	2 Tbsp. vegetable oil

Stir just enough to moisten dry ingredients.

Cook on skillet at medium-high heat. The skillet is ready when drops of water “dance” on it.

Chapter 12: Mastering the Art of Financial Well-Being: Strategies, Motivation, and Sustainable Habits

A. Recap of Key Strategies

In the grand tapestry of financial mastery, we've journeyed through a wealth of practical strategies to sculpt a secure and prosperous future. Let's recap the key strategies that form the foundation of your financial success:

B. Encouragement and Motivation

In the pursuit of financial freedom, resilience, and persistence are your allies. Remember, every small step you take today contributes to a brighter financial future tomorrow. Stay motivated by:

- **Embracing a Growth Mindset:**
    - View challenges as opportunities for growth. Learn from setbacks and use them as stepping stones to success.
- **Building a Support System:**
    - Surround yourself with a supportive community. Share your journey, learn from others, and stay inspired.

C. Looking Forward: Sustainable Financial Habits for the Future

As you gaze into the horizon of your financial future, consider cultivating sustainable habits that will stand the test of time:

- **Consistent Budgeting:**
    - Continue refining and adapting your budget as your financial landscape evolves.
- **Continuous Learning:**
    - Stay informed about personal finance trends and strategies. Knowledge is your greatest asset.
- **Teaching Others:**
    - Share your financial wisdom with friends and family. Empower others to embark on their journey to financial well-being.
- **Adapting to Change:**
    - Embrace flexibility and adaptability. Life is dynamic, and so too should be your financial strategies.

The path to financial freedom is not a destination but a continuous journey. Armed with knowledge, resilience, and a commitment to thoughtful choices, you are equipped to navigate the twists and turns of your financial expedition. As you step boldly into the future, remember:

Your financial destiny is in your hands, and every decision shapes the masterpiece of your financial legacy.

Chapter 13: Navigating Resources for Financial Mastery

A. Recommended Books and Articles

- Welcome to the treasure trove of resources designed to elevate your financial mastery. This chapter isn't just a list; it's a curated collection of tools, wisdom, and support services of efficiency, effectiveness, and maximum impact. Let's dive into the world of additional resources that will amplify your financial journey.
- **"The Total Money Makeover" by Dave Ramsey:**
    - Ramsey's practical advice and step-by-step plan provide a roadmap to financial peace.
- **"Your Money or Your Life" by Vicki Robin and Joe Dominguez:**
    - A transformative guide that redefines your relationship with money and empowers you to achieve financial independence.
- **"The Simple Path to Wealth" by J.L. Collins:**
    - Collins distills the complexities of investing into straightforward principles, making wealth-building accessible to all.

- **"Atomic Habits" by James Clear:**
    - Clear's insights on habits offer a powerful framework for creating positive financial behaviors.
- **"The Millionaire Next Door" by Thomas J. Stanley and William D. Danko:**
    - A revealing exploration of the habits and characteristics of millionaires, providing valuable lessons for building wealth.
- **"The 4-Hour Workweek" by Timothy Ferriss:** Delve into Ferriss's blueprint for creating more with less. Learn to optimize your time and resources for maximum impact.

B. Online Tools and Apps for Budgeting

Harness the power of technology to streamline your financial journey. Here are some online tools and apps to assist you in budgeting and financial planning:

- **Mint:**
    - An all-in-one app for budgeting, expense tracking, and financial goal setting.
- **YNAB (You Need A Budget):**

- A budgeting tool that focuses on giving every dollar a job, ensuring intentional spending.

- **Personal Capital:**
    - A comprehensive platform that offers budgeting, investment tracking, and retirement planning features.
- **PocketGuard:**
    - A user-friendly app that helps you track spending, set savings goals, and stay within budget.
- **EveryDollar:**
    - Dave Ramsey's budgeting tool is designed to make budgeting straightforward and efficient.

C. Financial Counseling and Support Services

Sometimes, seeking guidance from financial experts can provide the clarity needed to navigate complex financial landscapes. Explore the following financial counseling and support services:

- **National Foundation for Credit Counseling (NFCC):**
    - NFCC offers counseling and education on budgeting, credit, and debt management.

- **Financial Counseling Association of America (FCAA):**
    - FCAA provides access to certified financial counselors for personalized guidance.
- **Smart About Money (SAM):**
    - SAM offers free online courses and resources to enhance your financial knowledge.
- **Local Community Services:**
    - Explore local community resources for financial counseling and support. Many communities have nonprofit organizations that assist.

3. Investing Wisdom:

- **"The Little Book of Common Sense Investing" by John C. Bogle:** A guide to simple, low-cost investing strategies that have stood the test of time.
- **"Rich Dad Poor Dad" by Robert T. Kiyosaki:** A paradigm-shifting exploration of financial education and the difference between working for money and making money work for you.

4. **Financial Psychology:**

- **"Nudge" by Richard H. Thaler and Cass R. Sunstein:** Understand the subtle ways in which our decisions are influenced and how to make better financial choices.
- **"The Psychology of Money" by Morgan Housel:** Dive into the psychological nuances that shape our relationship with money and impact our financial decisions.

2. **Investment Management:**

- **Robinhood:** A user-friendly platform for commission-free investing in stocks, ETFs, and cryptocurrencies.
- **Acorns:** Invest spare change automatically, turning everyday purchases into a diversified portfolio.

3. **Savings and Goal Planning:**

- **Qapital:** Automate savings based on your goals and preferences, making saving money a seamless part of your lifestyle.
- **Digit:** An intelligent savings app that analyzes your spending habits and saves money for you in small, manageable increments.

6. **Credit Monitoring and Management:**

- **Credit Karma:** Monitor your credit score, receive credit reports, and get personalized tips for improving your credit health.

7. **Financial Counseling and Support Services**

- **Bankrate:** Access financial calculators www.bankrate.com
- **SmartAsset:** Access financial calculators, tools, and content to make informed financial decisions.
- **National Foundation for Credit Counseling (NFCC):** Connect with certified financial counselors for personalized advice on budgeting, debt management, and more.

8. **Community and Support Groups:**

- **Financial Independence Reddit (r/financialindependence):** A supportive community discussing various aspects of financial independence, early retirement, and smart financial planning.

9. **Educational Platforms:**

For personal finance classes, learning employment skills and personal interest.

- **Khan Academy**

- **Coursera**
- **Alison**
- **Udemy**
- **Harvard Online Courses**

10. Financial Calculators:

- **Bankrate (bankrate.com):** Bankrate offers a variety of financial calculators, including those for mortgages, auto loans, credit cards, and more.

Mobile Apps:

- **Financial Calculators (by Bishinews):** This is a popular financial calculator app available for both Android and iOS devices.
- **BA Financial Calculator (by Ernest Brock):** Another app available for Android and iOS, offering various financial functions.

Built-in Calculators:

- **Excel/Google Sheets:** You can also use spreadsheet software like Microsoft Excel or Google Sheets to create your own financial calculators. They often have built-in functions for financial calculations.

Cookbooks (remember you can look up their YouTube channels and blogs to get free recipes)

- "Be A Plant-Based Woman Warrior: Live Fierce, Stay Bold, Eat Delicious"
  "Prevent and Reverse Heart Disease Cookbook" by Ann Crile Esselstyn and Jane Esselstyn
- "Plantifully Lean: 125+ Simple and Satisfying Plant-Based Recipes for Health and Weight Loss" by Kiki Reader Nelson
- "Plant Based Cooking Made Easy: Over 100 Recipes" by Jill Dalton
- "How Not to Die Cookbook" by Dr. Michael Greger and Gene Stone
- "Mastering Diabetes" by Cyrus Khambatta and Robby Barbaro
- "Unprocessed" by Chef AJ
- "The Starch Solution" by John A. McDougall
- "Forks Over Knives - The Cookbook" by Del Sroufe
- "The Engine 2 Cookbook" by Rip Esselstyn

- "The Vegan 8" by Brandi Doming

  Simple recipes with eight ingredients or less

A couple of website for people that do not have their books on Amazon but I thought you would like their recipes:

- https://www.thejaroudifamily.com/recipes
- https://www.brandnewvegan.com/

Conclusion: A Wealth of Wisdom at Your Fingertips

In conclusion, these resources are not just tools; they are your companions on the journey to financial mastery. As you navigate the complexities of personal finance, remember that knowledge is your greatest asset. Explore, learn, and implement the strategies that resonate with you. This chapter is not just an endpoint; it's a Launchpad for continuous growth and financial excellence. Welcome to the era where knowledge empowers, tools amplify, and your financial journey unfolds with precision and impact.

References: Behind the Curtain: The Wizards of Wisdom

Note: Most sources for this book are based on general principles and widely accepted financial advice.

1. Stanley, T. J., & Danko, W. D. (1996). The Millionaire Next Door: The surprising Secrets of America's Wealthy. Taylor Trade Publishing.
2. Covey, S. R. (2005). The 7 Habits of Highly Effective People: Personal Workbook. COVEY.
3. Alison | Free online courses & online learning. (n.d.). Alison. https://alison.com
4. Mortgage calculator. (n.d.). Mortgage Calculator. https://www.mortgagecalculator.org
5. Bank Rate. (n.d.). Bankrate: Guiding you through life's financial journey. Bankrate. https://bankrate.com/
6. Bingham, Rita, Country Beans - How to cook dry beans in only 3 minutes! (2011). Country Beans - How to cook dry beans in only 3 minutes! Natural Health Solutions
7. OpenAI's GPT-3.5 model, January 2024

Thank you for taking the time to read this book. I trust you discovered valuable insights that you can apply.
If you found the content beneficial, I would greatly appreciate it if you could consider leaving a positive review.

Beth Holm, beelovedholm@gmail.com

Month

Family Expenses

Expenses	Amount Paid
Mortgage or Rent	
Car Payment	
Gas	
Car Maintenance	
Auto Insurance	
Public Transportation	
Health Insurance	
Out-Of-Pocket Medical Costs	
Life Insurance	

Month

Family Expenses

Expenses	Amount Paid
Electricity	
Natural Gas	
Water	
Sanitation/Garbage	
Internet	
Phone	
Groceries Toiletries	
Personal Care	
Haircuts	
Child Care	
Credit Cards	
Student Loans	
Other Loans	

Month

Family Expenses

Expenses	Amount Paid

Personal Expenses

Expenses	Cost

Personal Expenses

Expenses	Cost

Needs	Wants

Needs	Wants

Subscriptions

Can we cancel any?

Fun Thing to do as a Family

What I Want to Learn

New Foods to Try

Things we are Saving For

Made in the USA
Monee, IL
04 November 2026

67377406R00059